Yes, my Photos are Fake – and Why I do it

Catfishing in the First Person

This book is written as somewhat of a cautionary tale on the many issues derived from seeking online relationships. Of course there are already many other books on the same subject, but – as far as I know – there is none actually defending the practise which is nowadays often called *catfishing*. And that's what this book is all about, an attempt of showing the other side of the topic, of presenting the truth about such a practise, showing general readers that it is not all about, let's say, a 52-year-old man sitting in their parent's basement and conning young children, or a 200 Kg woman stuck at home and hidden behind Instagram filters, or even a horrible monster attempting to mislead others for personal gain while laughing maniacally in his mother's basement.

Simply put, nowadays I use photos which are not my own on social media and on a popular online dating app. I have absolutely no problem about admitting it – in fact, a phrase in my profile may typically warn readers that there's one lie on my page, with its most recent version clearly stating "I promise to tell you a single lie, but quite a worthy one". Naturally, I would later disclose the "single lie" I am telling before going out with someone. In fact, it felt completely necessary to do so, because my point was never the one tricking others, but instead following an unusual pattern that I feel is quite understandable, and which serves a very particular goal, one that will become perfectly clear across the pages of this book.

But then, one night in November 2019, I went out with a girl named Tatiana. I had previously told her "You know my photos are fake, right?", and she appeared to confirm that she knew it all along. And yet, when we went out, she seemed... perhaps shocked at seeing me. She didn't know what to say, and I felt completely horrible about it, because I had (apparently?) tricked her into going out with me, when that was never my goal at all. Maybe I hadn't been clear enough, when I revealed my usage of fake photos? I'm not sure, maybe I wasn't, despite my attempt to, but that still deeply upset me. What I do was never about tricking people, and yet there I was, feeling horrible about it, apologizing profusely, and I honestly felt – and feel – bad about it. As an atonement of sorts, I promised her I'd write this book.

And, in its kernel, this is what this book is all about – my personal story on why I use "fake" photos online. For once, you can get to read the true story behind all of this, why I do what I do – and, perhaps as importantly, *why you should, too!*

Index

1- How this all thing started

Maybe I should start by saying that I was never someone interested in meeting many other people. I couldn't care any less about casual relationships either. And I am not a complete asshole, nor do I particularly enjoy tricking people. And, believe it or not, I do not even lack self-confidence. Instead, what first led me to social media and online relationships was a mere common interest in human relationships, and why we sometimes act the way we do in our lives.

At the time, I had met a woman named Helena and we had become best friends. We spent almost all our free time together. She was the most amazing person I met in my life, and yet... my heart was crushed when she told me that, until the age of 20-something years old, when she met me, she had never had a single friend in her life, simply because she looked different. Here she was, a person who was almost a complete genius, already undertaking a PhD in her early twenties, and yet people were, as she used to put it, "complete assholes just because I have short hair, small breasts and often dress manly".

We could not understand this, at all. If meeting another human being was all about connecting on a deeper level, why were people acting like this towards her, all her life? How could I be there, looking at, and talking, to this absolutely amazing human being, feeling that nobody else in this world could be by my side like she was, and yet accept that others had always been such enormous jerks towards her?

While (painfully) debating this subject, we went for several long walks. We would just walk and walk, in the middle of the night, while sharing several potential theories regarding this problem, until we came up with a potential thesis – were looks all that people cared about, nowadays? Two people being the same in everything else, would a cute one be nicely treated, while a potentially not-so-cute one be discarded away, almost as if she was not even a real human being at all? Such a possibility was definitely scary, grotesque, profoundly sad, and so we decided we had to know the truth about it. However, we also felt it was very difficult to test such a possibility;

realistically speaking, we could not make one of us consistently cuter – or uglier – solely to test this hypothesis. Even if we could, ultimately it would not be possible to replicate all the conditions of the experience multiple times, and that would naturally taint the results. Our conceptual answers, even if we could find some way to test them in "real life", would always end up suffering from methodological issues, and would always provide others with the basic scapegoat of claiming that we didn't replicate *all* the same elements of the experiment for *all* the different people involved in it.

Again and again, we tried to come up with an alternative. Fortunately – or perhaps it is more accurate to say *unfortunately*? – we ended up finding a sort of solution – even if we could not test our potential theory in our daily lives, we could attempt an adapted version of it through online media, since that would increase the variables we could actually control.

Since mobile apps still weren't a thing back then, we started by checking what were the most popular online dating and social media websites in our country. We created a small listing containing all of those, checked which unique features were available in each of them, and then noticed there was a key component we likely needed for our experiment – message receipts, which would allow us to verify whether other people had actually read our messages or not; otherwise, we could simply end up waiting "eternally" for a message that would never come.

For this reason, we started by tracking which websites had such a "message receipts" feature. For each one of those, we created an empty account and tried to verify how many people were 25 Km away from our location. Although this may seem like a very small search radius, it should be noted that we live near our country's capital city, and so we hoped this would give us a fair number of people for our experiment. For that reason, we ended up simply picking the website with the higher number of active people in our area.

By now, I'm almost sure you're curious about what specific website we ended up picking. Human beings are curious by nature, and I myself would be wondering about it, if I was reading about this initial experiment, too. However, for legal reasons I cannot present you that information – what I can tell you is that the website remains active nowadays, now it also has a dating app associated with it, and as of the time of the writing of these lines claims to have over 400000000 active users – that's four hundred million people, more than the entire population of the USA, and approximately 5% of the world's current population.

But let's proceed with the report regarding our experiment. We then decided to create two different accounts in this same website, both of them with precisely all the same basic textual information. In theory, and given these controlled conditions, people would be equally interested in any of the two. They would have no real reasons, at all, to prefer one over the other. And so, the only difference between them would be a photo. Each profile would feature just one photo, a single and very temporary snapshot of one person's entire lifetime.

But... what photos could we use? Even if we

decided to take some random images from some online profile and use them as our own, we felt it would be difficult to control some side factors – such as the person's position, photo location, look, smiling face, etc. – as any of the images extensively available would never be precisely what we needed for our experiment. For that reason, we ended up using... *me* (!), the author of these lines, as the proverbial guinea pig.

First, we took a photo of myself, precisely as I wake up in the morning, and added it to the profile I will here call "Turtle", over the famous fable of Aesop[1]. There was nothing specially noteworthy about this one photo, it was just me as I wake up in the morning.

Next, we decided to completely pimp me up. A few minutes later we took a second photo, this one with me impeccably well dressed, a great pose, smiling, and so on. We also edited out any potential flaws with a photo editing software. Honestly, I should admit we tried everything we could to make this one image as perfect as possible; we could not change

_____

1   Evidently, these names were not used for any of the profiles.

who I really was, physically, but through the magic of angles, illusions and *Photoshop* we could, ultimately, make me much better looking than I usually am, and significantly different from the previous photo. Now, for the same reason as above, let's call this second profile "Hare".

In a very natural way, we quickly took both "Turtle" and "Hare" for a spin. We went to talk to the same 100 people, picked at random, with both profiles, and we approached each of them with precisely the same introductory phrase, a simple "Hey there, how's it going?" In our view, since both profiles featured the same information and approached everyone in the exact same way, this would ensure that if people contacted us, it would all be down to the photo in itself, their only distinguishing element. And so, given these conditions, "Turtle" was contacted back 5 times (although many more people did read its original message), while "Hare" was answered to 93 times (by the time we finished the experiment, everyone who had read the original message had replied to it).

Now, if you're curious about it, nobody contacted just the first profile. Out of the five people who contacted both, one of them told "Turtle" she answered messages slowly because she was busy working at the time – but, at the very same moments, she always used to answer "Hare" almost instantly. Another person seemed to enjoy talking to both, but unexpectedly mocked "Turtle" to "Hare", pointing out how horrible that other profile looked. And, for better and for worse, this part of the experiment seemed to prove the famous adage that says that "looks matter".

Right now, while reading these lines, I am certain that at least a few readers are saying to themselves "Wow, these two young fellows proved that *looks matter*! What a big deal, but everyone already knows that!" In retrospective, they would be absolutely right. Perhaps, by this experiment, we were simply attempting to reinvent the wheel, as the saying goes. But facing these results, we then decided to go for a new walk and debated how to proceed. Out of "Turtle" and "Hare", of course people preferred the most attractive profile, because at the time we were mostly testing the attractiveness of a single snapshot.

And, for that reason, we could not help but wonder what would happen if we could infuse "Hare" with an absolutely horrible personality.

"Turtle" got nowhere, as the five people who had initially messaged such profile soon stopped answering back, and so we decided to delete that profile. We then proceeded with the "Hare" profile alone – I guess the turtle doesn't always win the race, does it?[2] – and we decided to try to test what would happen if, despite being attractive, that profile was also the most horrible person we could think of. Essentially, this required asking some women in our lives about what they desired the most in a men, and then completely inverting the answers we got. Long story short, we decided to turn him married (and a notorious cheater!), with very young children, abusive towards his wife and kids, completely misogynistic, homophobic, racist, a sex maniac, a near-constant liar, unemployed out of his own personal option (and still living with his physically sick parents, which he repeatedly treated as slaves), and so on. But if this supposed personality still wasn't bad enough, we also

---

2   Sorry about the silly pun, *I just had to*!

tried to make him say the most horrible things we could think of. And I'm sure most readers will be somewhat curious about this, and so let me provide just three quick examples.

We would randomly stop talking to people in the middle of a continuous conversation, blame them for this, and then turn completely abusive and insulting if they themselves took more than a single minute to answer us back. Soon enough, people started *apologizing* for not being able to answer us quicker, as if they had done something wrong, even when they evidently hadn't. And yet, *zero* people stopped talking to us over it.

Also, we would claim we had put a two-month old baby alone in a bathtub filled with water, followed by completely rude and abusive phrases such as "If he dies, he dies. I never wanted him anyway, that whore got pregnant from someone else and said it was mine!" One would naturally hope this would completely horrify people, and yet *zero* people stopped talking to us over it.

Finally, we would invent an episode in which we had brutally assaulted our wife, because we had supposedly seen her talking to someone else near a cross walk. We would describe the incident with the most vivid details we could think of, again hoping to horrify people, and yet *zero* people stopped talking to us over it. In fact, at least one person went as far as laughing and replying "That's good. If you told her that you don't want her to talk to anyone else, and she still does it... that's clearly because she doesn't respect you. But I would!"

At this point, I must admit some of these details may seem rather shocking. They may seem so horrible that one could expect or wish them not to be true. "How can they be true?", at least one reader is certainly asking itself. And, in all the honesty available to me in this world, I can guarantee you this all happened as presented here. In fact, and simply put, this even shows why people stay in abusive relationships; why people often don't act when they see a couple involved in an episode of domestic violence; and perhaps even why the murder of young children is often taken so lightly by the Law when one of the potential parents is undoubtedly and repeatedly abusive.

All things considered, the results we obtained with this second part of our experiment scared us very much. Because the "Turtle" profile did not have a beautiful photo, it was essentially ignored, people wouldn't even make any effort in establishing a relationship with it; at the same time, the "Hare" one, with a beautiful photo, was extensively talked to, and regardless of how abusively it behaved, people just wouldn't stop talking to it!

Soon, we had to drop the entire experiment, as it was heavily affecting us at a psychological level. We now knew that looks mattered, but what deeply upset us was that if a profile's photo – or the human being behind it – was attractive enough, it could get away with pretty much anything. I'll even say it again – even if "Turtle" was the most amazing human being who had ever lived, nobody talked to him based on his photo; at the same time, "Hare" could be a complete asshole, but people would still talk to him solely based on his attractiveness. And, for this reason, it truly seemed that Helena was being treated badly solely based on her unusual looks, which deeply saddened us.

But, if you want to consider that our results were mere exceptions, that people just can't be all that bad, you can simply go online nowadays and read about many other similar experiments performed in the last few years, often with results very similar to these. From an attractive male model (and child molester), to an abusive man on ankle monitor, along with guys who tried to be as creepy as possible, there are all kinds of experiments that mirror these same results, and that say something horribly frightening about today's online relationship culture – as another writer best put it, its essential rules seem to be extremely simple, and they all go around the idea of "be attractive, and don't be ugly".

2- But looks matter in "real life" too, right?

A quick opposition to this problem could be raised by stressing that people's looks matter in "real life", too. And of course they do, that's impossible to deny. But the big difference between online relationships and those established in our daily lives is that, when it comes down to meeting other people face to face, looks are only one component of the whole process, one that tends to vary depending on what, specifically, you may be looking for in your life. If, for example, you are merely looking for someone who shares your love for *Harry Potter* books, the way that person looks certainly ranks low in your scale; if, however, your current goal is the one of finding yourself a hiking partner, it seems completely natural to require that such a person is, at the very least, fit enough to be able to accompany you in those journeys. And, of course, if you're both looking for some casual sex, caring exclusively about someone's looks ends up being perfectly reasonable.

Realistically, we are all looking for something in

our lives. Even if we are already married, or have children, or in the middle of a completely stable relationship, there are significant chances that we still don't feel completely happy and fulfilled with what we have. For that reason, if we are taking a bus home, and someone who is really nice sits by our side and establishes a conversation with us, chances are that we won't shut them down, unless their goals seem to be completely different from what we are looking for in a particular point of our lives – if you're married and have children, and you really love your partner, chances are that someone who establishes a conversation with you and quickly starts telling you how beautiful you are, and then asks you about your relationship status, may have very different goals from your own.

At the same time, however, if you just randomly meet a great person in the middle of the street, and you have a great dialogue, it is likely that you don't really care about the way they look – unless they're actual monsters, with tentacles and fangs, I'd have to assume. You can simply add one more person to your life and see where that takes you, even if your common interests are not the ones of potentially dating each other. And, if you think more about it, you'll end up quickly noticing this is a middle ground which exists in all human relationships – not everyone in the world is looking for a long-term relationship or casual sex!

For example, I once sat on a train station's bench for a few minutes. An older woman, at least 80 years old, soon sat by my side, and we happily talked about random stuff for a few minutes, until the next train came to the station. Naturally, we both had no other goal besides simply sitting there and sharing a little bit of our lives with each other – and that's perfectly okay! However, such middle ground does not seem to exist in online interactions, almost as if we expected everyone else to be looking *solely* for an intimate romantic (or sexual) relationship with us.

A noteworthy example of this problem can be found in another popular online dating app and website. When you first create your account, you're allowed to select whether you're "single", "seeing someone" or "married". There's no other option, you have to fit into one of those three categories, almost as if your entire life could simply be placed into one of those three baskets. But what if you're single and not really looking to date? What if you were already married before, and you're now a widower? What if you simply want someone to accompany you to local art exhibitions – why should your relationship status, and theirs, even matter for that? For such reasons, I did contact that place's customer support, gave them these suggestions, they openly admitted they were great and made perfect sense, and yet... nothing ever came out of it, even after a few years, which only shows how interested they are in improving their product.

Following the question on your relationship status, you're then asked to pick what you're looking for – "new friends", a "long-term relationship", a "short-term relationship", or "casual sex". When creating a profile, naturally I would only select I was looking for "new friends", for reasons that will become clear in the next chapter, and yet... time and again, since I hadn't ticked any of the two available "... relationship" boxes, I would be asked if selecting only "new friends" meant that I was just looking for the proverbial "friends with benefits". I wasn't, and it was a bit unsettling to notice that most people were assuming so by default.

Simply put, this is absurd. Not everyone in this world has to be looking for a relationship and/or sex. Can't two human beings, regardless of their gender, simply want to talk to each other, learn from one another, exclusively sit on a park bench and talk for hours and hours? And, assuming such basic goal, why should people's looks matter, if at all? If someone naturally strikes a conversation with us in the middle of the street, we don't usually care about their looks, and yet... this basic assumption is very different, when it comes down to a relationship established online – "be attractive, and don't be ugly", or you'll go nowhere at all.

3- Why I started using fake photos

In the first chapter I told you about Helena, and how much I cared about her. But what I didn't tell you before is that I lost her in early 2015. There's not much point in talking about her death here, but having lost her I soon found myself in a very dark place. How could I, as a human being, understand and accept that I had met such an amazing person, but now had to live the rest of my life without her by my side ever again? How could I tell myself that I had once met this one woman, who was essentially everything I had always looked for, and then I had lost her? Anyone who has faced a similar situation certainly knows how painful it all is.

For months, I struggled with this new problem. No psychologist, no meditation, no knowledge of the "Four Noble Truths", could help me, until one day I came across a copy of Marcus Tullius Cicero's *De Senectute*[3], which taught me that what happened to

---

3   Best known among English speakers as his treatise "On Old Age".

her, although painful to me, was only natural. "Was she not a mortal?", Cicero asks. Of course she was, as all of us are, and despite not bringing her back, the lessons from such book allowed me to understand that I had to keep on going through my journey of life.

Some months later I decided I was ready to meet new people. But, soon enough, I found myself facing quite an unusual problem – I was not exactly desperate for a new relationship, I simply wanted to meet new people, take things slow, and see where that would take us in the long run. Although I met some people in "real life", again and again I felt that we often did not share the same interests. In fact, people would frequently look at me as if I was some kind of mythological creature, just because I had actually read the works of Cicero (among many other classical authors and works, from Homer and the *Epic of Gilgamesh* to Boethius, Dante, Petrarch and Voltaire). Time and again, I was told that mine was likely a dying breed in today's world.

Facing this issue, how was I to find someone who shared my interests? How was I to find another human being who, instead of wanting to quickly jump in a new relationship, or having sex with me by the third date, would first and foremost desire to establish a potential long-term friendship based on our common interests? Naturally assuming I was not some sort of last unicorn, I supposed I was not alone in this unusual search, and I decided that going online would raise the chance of finding what I sought. And so, I soon started looking for somebody else who shared my personal interests.

After the experiment we had once performed, and which I detailed extensively in the first chapter, this was the very first time I joined social media and attempted to use an online dating app. I tried all my best to create a good profile, based on what we once had learned, and soon enough I was browsing a few profiles. I didn't really care about people's looks, I would just browse each individual profile, one by one, and read what they all said. Here and there, I ended up finding people who deeply intrigued me, from a person who appeared to have shared some of my experiences in life, to that one girl who expressed a major interest in classical literature herself; I found people who wanted to learn more about obscure literature[4], fellow human beings who also sought to learn new things on a daily basis (like I do), and so on. And yet, even if I was completely honest with all of those people, I would seldom get an answer back. I did not know if they had actually read my messages – unfortunately, the app I was using lacked such a feature – but their repeated and significant lack of replies astonished me.

Was I *that* ugly in my natural photos, as the original experiment had once shown? I tried some better photos, and yet the same problem subsisted. I was deeply intrigued by this, not knowing what I was doing wrong, until one woman asked me two extremely eye-opening questions – "Is your profile fake? Why do you have photos of a young teen in it?"

At the time I was already over 30 years old, and those photos I presented people in my page had been taken during my latest journey, one to Pamplona, Spain. Naturally, the images I was showing people were not "fake" in any way, they were my own, and

---

4   In the sense of books that people seldom read nowadays.

they presented me as I looked less than two or three years prior. And yet, then further inquiring other people about this, they seemed to feel the same – they thought my profile was just a fake one, because they assumed it was not me in any of the photos.

Did I look *that* younger? This kind of thing is always open for debate, but I should explain that 13 months after Helena's death it was found out that I have an auto-immune disease. One of its symptoms appears to be an overproduction of collagen, i.e. the famous protein frequently used in beauty creams. Apparently, this makes me age much slower than usual, which easily explains why, whenever I see friends from my high school days, they always tell me I appear not to have aged a single day over the years.

Realistically, what was I to do about this? As a doctor once put it, "Well, you should see the positive side, you'll never have any wrinkles in your face". If I had ever cared about my own looks – something I had stopped doing after being traumatized by the experiment described in a previous chapter – this would definitely be a great asset, but at that point in time it seemed like a very real issue. In spite of the fact everyone I knew appeared to call me "the most interesting man I have ever met", I could not age myself artificially. I could not make myself look older, and that seemed to impede the task of establishing any online relationships.

"First-world problems", right? So many people eagerly wishing to look younger all their lives, and there I was, complaining about the exact opposite. At the time, I did not know how to solve this issue, but it certainly bothered me. I had already travelled all over the world seeking knowledge, I was making way more money than I needed, I had already published several books (including a best seller), I had won some awards, I had gone through a few college degrees, I was an active volunteer for welfare projects, and yet... everything people seemed to care about, online, were my looks, and the unusual fact that I looked much younger than I really was.

In the short run, this even led me to a very strange issue – people would look at my photos and say I looked very young, and then they would talk to me and *again* assume my profile was fake, this time based on the fact that due to all the knowledge I have I could not be thirty-something years old – I evidently had to be much older, or so they claimed. If this seems a bit confusing to you, well, I must openly admit I too was confused by it. How was it possible for me to cumulatively look younger and feel older to others? Again, I did not know what to make out of this, but something quite unexpected occurred – despite the fact some people were telling me that through my knowledge I seemed older, they horizontally admitted they were enjoying the constant dialogues they were having with me.

And, to be completely honest, across time I too found myself enjoying the dialogues I had with those people, even if sometimes they were not entirely what I was looking for. Some of them are still my friends to this day, and they are perfectly aware of everything written in this book. In spite of that, whenever I found people I truly wanted to talk to, more often than not I would never hear back from them, and that made me sad, because I felt I would really connect very well with some of those people.

And so... this whole situation first led me to use other people's photos as my own. How I selected them is a subject for the next chapter, but for now all that matters is that I felt the problem I was facing could be worked around if I simply looked older. And, strangely enough, this strategy worked. Soon, I was able to strike real dialogues with some of the people I truly wanted to get to know better. At the same time, this also led me to an equally unavoidable question – how was I expected to get to know them in "real life"? How could I tell them "You've been talking to this guy, and you've been enjoying his virtual company, but the photos you saw are not from him, and here's why"?

4- Wait, wait! Why did you select those specific photos?

Since, based on the problem discussed in the previous chapter, I was now using photos that did not belong to me, a crucial question must definitely be answered – why did I select *those* specific photos? I didn't really care about other people's looks, but was I not afraid of leading people to talk to me exclusively based on the content of my own "improved" photos?

Well, at the time I had already decided this was my only option, for the aforementioned reasons. I could not make myself look older, at least not consistently and without much continuous effort. And so, I went through some popular photo websites, grabbed some images from a random guy who appeared to be my age and height, significantly changed their internal content (otherwise, they would be easily tracked down through image-lookup websites), and presented them as my own. However – and I should stress this very clearly – my point was never the one of misleading people about the kind of things I typically do in my daily life and in my free time. For that reason, I also quickly decided I could, and would, only present photos which pictured my own (and real) personal experiences.

Perhaps this is best explained with a few examples. In the north of Spain there is a really beautiful small town called Santillana del Mar, which I once visited, and so I presented people with a photo taken in front of its beautiful monastery, my back turned to the camera. I attend many conferences as a lecturer, and so another photo would show "me" impeccably well dressed in one of those events. I visit many medieval locations for my research, and a third photo would naturally show "me" in an old medieval church. I like animals, and so another photo would place "me" just next to a horse or cuddling a few goats. I love backpacking, and for that reason you'd also be able to see "me" doing exactly that. I have the habit of meditating by riversides – and there's another photo showing that, too. And so, essentially, the photos I presented people would really show the kind of thing I typically do in my life, with the only difference being that the person shown in them was not really me.

Why did I feel this was crucial? Because, as I already stressed above, I did not want to mislead people about my own personal experiences. I did not want anyone to see my profile and tell me "Oh, there's a photo of you skydiving, that's one of my big passions too". I did not want to press potential friendships with any other lies from the get-go; instead, I always promised myself I would tell people *a single lie*, *just one*, and that was always about the photos I was using as my own, and nothing else.

But, naturally, this led me to same issue hinted at near the end of the previous chapter – since I did not want to perpetuate a purely virtual connection until the end of time, how would I be able to, eventually, tell people the truth? How would I be able to explain them that they had been speaking with a real human being all along, and that everything they had been reading when talking to me was completely true, barring the photos?

5- Don't you wonder about the truth behind other people?

Based on the previous chapters, I felt I had a strong reason to use "fake" photos, but I was still unsure on how I would be able to, eventually, reveal people the truth. That was completely necessary, since I did not want to prolong a virtual relationship forever. But how could I tell them, how could I make them understand my whole point? The answer soon came to me, almost by complete accident.

For a moment imagine yourself in a long-term relationship. It's all going great, but how can you be sure that this one person will really be there for you in the future? How can you be sure that you're not being two timed? How can you know this person is not with you only for the money, or out of some other kind of self-interest alone? And wouldn't you like to know? Wouldn't you really like to know the truth behind other people? Across the years I asked questions such as these to a very large number of people, and their answer was a horizontal and very resounding "yes, I would obviously like to know!" Imagine how many broken hearts would have been avoided if you had known what this or that person *really* wanted from you in the first place!

Back when we did the second part of the original experiment, one of our side-findings made us laugh quite a bit. Not only were people building a virtual reality by coming up with excuses to explain away, and make way more acceptable, issues as serious as domestic violence and potential murder, but they were also frequently lying to us. We assumed this was happening because, by doing so, people would be able to generate more interest in them. Some of the cases we went through, back then, were as absurd as a woman telling us that the *Margites* was one of her favourite books. In case you have never heard of it before, this is "just" a poem ascribed to the legendary poet Homer, and which was lost over 1000 years ago (and, for that reason, she naturally couldn't have read it at all). It is likely that, because we had just mentioned that one book, she felt that by presenting herself as having read it, we would think highly of her and become more interested in getting to know her.

A way to go around this problem, of people lying to you just because they find you attractive, would naturally be the one of presenting my real photos, but as described in a previous chapter that was not really an option in my case – people would, as before, think it was not me in the photos, and discard me away as if I had a "fake" profile.

Facing such an issue, and as part of a complete accident, I soon noticed that my usage of those "fake" photos was giving me an accidental, and also totally unplanned, way to test the actual truth behind people. Here I was, talking to other people. Here they were, enjoying the conversations they were having with me. And, in theory, if those people were truly enjoying my (virtual) company, the fact the photos were not mine would have mattered little to them. I mean, realistically, I would still be me, I was still the same person they had been talking to all along. And, theoretically, this makes a lot sense – would *you* want to know that someone is talking to you just because of the way you look? Even if looks matter, shouldn't they only be a sparse component of any potential relationship?

That's why I always felt the need to tell people about what I was doing, sooner or later, before going out with them, because I did not want to mislead them. I wanted them to know the whole thing, and decide how to act accordingly. Maybe that's why Tatiana's case upset me so much – I had told her, and yet she appeared to feel that I hadn't been good enough at doing so, and due to that weakness I ended up accidentally tricking her and causing us to go out when she was expecting one thing and ended up getting a very different one. And that was quite unfortunate. However, on a more general level, when I revealed the complete truth to people, one out of three things tended to happen:

Some people would suddenly stop talking to me. I was perfectly comfortable and okay with this, because they acting in such a way showed me what they were really interested in – and it wasn't me! You can attempt to come up with a thousand polite excuses for their behaviour, but the honest truth is that if you're talking to someone and, upon telling them X they stop talking to you, it is quite easy to realize they did it because of you having told them X. And, no matter how many excuses they attempt to choose to explain away their behaviour, the truth is that they were just complete jerks who only cared about looks – it's as simple as that!

Other people did not stop talking to me, but either tried to rush me into going out with them (likely expecting to see who I really was), or suddenly started talking to me *less and less* – like what happened to Tatiana, who after meeting me said she still wanted to talk to me, but then lowered the "constant messages" ratio to "less than ten" in the next day, and then went for a "I forgot my phone home yesterday, sorry" on the second, and then completely stopped texting me[5]. There are many potential ways to explain people's new behaviour, ranging from completely bad to fairly acceptable ones, but overall I felt that, deep inside, they just weren't *that* into me and our dialogues in the first place. Although this may seem more acceptable

---

5   And no, I should stress nothing wrong happened. Instead, she had texted me, and as I came home I answered it, she read my reply and... never answered back, even after I contacted her twice.

than the previous case, it is equally possible they were attempting to artificially kill our connection, following something along the lines of "I will simply talk to him less; he'll soon learn his tacit lesson, and then stop talking to me on his own". Such technique would allow them to preserve their self-image, not having to admit to themselves – or to me – they were just talking to another person over some beautiful images.

But, unexpectedly, a third group continued to talk to me just as before. Some of them went as far as telling me they couldn't care less about my photos, and that they genuinely enjoying talking to me. And that was what I had been looking for all along.

Although this whole idea may seem unusual, one should be reminded I have an auto-immune disease. That's genetic, not curable, and usually degenerative. All doctors can do is slowing down its progress. Based on that, even if I was to search for someone who finds me attractive the way I look right now, chances are that across time, as my physical status worsens, they'd find some internally-acceptable way to abandon me. Although people generally aren't assholes enough to tell others "Bye, I liked you back in the day, but your disease's progression changed that!", an interesting aspect of the human condition, one I realized across the years, is that people tend to come up with many excuses to explain away a behaviour, no matter how horrible their actions may seem to those looking from the outside.

As a famous TV character used to say, "People lie". They'll lie a thousand times, if that's what it takes for them to reach some internal goal they have. I myself lie, *once*, the reasons explained in this book. But, if it takes that one lie to find out the actual truth that hides behind other people, and whether they wanted to talk to the real me (as opposed to just a bunch of fancy photos), I am perfectly comfortable with it.

6- Why should you do the same?

As I was writing a previous chapter from this book, something worth mentioning happened. I had recently matched with someone in a random dating app, and as usual I sent her my initial message – "Hey [name here]. How did your day go?" – but despite having read it, she did not write me back. More than a day later, I sent her a second message – "Wow, are you always this talkative?" – and once again the message was read but not replied to. After a period of three days had elapsed, a message from the same person finally appeared – "Hey there. I'm sorry, I don't come here very often". Of course she was lying, I knew she had read the previous messages, but I decided to play along and push further into the subject with a whole new question – "[name here], that's a shame, how will anyone be able to get to know you like that?"

Her answer stunned me – "They have to be patient, like a puppy waiting for its owner to come back. Otherwise, they're not worth it." These two phrases, in my view, capture perfectly the problem about online relationships of our days. As a man, you'll only be talked to if you're specially attractive, and even if you fulfil that (now somewhat "basic") requirement, you're then frequently treated as a worthless commodity, in the sense that if you don't want to follow the arbitrary rules women will tend to set for you, there'll be a huge number of other men perfectly willing – or, as one may jokingly add, *desperately wanting* – to pay attention to them, while very obediently wagging their tail when they're requested to.

From a human standpoint, this game of sorts is horrible, because it inflates a woman's value, no matter how worthless she is (and trust me, there are some really bad ones out there, like that one girl who threw her newborn baby on the trash, then took a selfie and added it to *Instagram* under the hashtag #takingtrashout), while at the same time diminishing the worth of all men, almost as if they were mere toys instead of real human beings. In my personal case, and even with fake photos on my profile[6], I found

---

6   Without those, people wouldn't even talk to me, or I'd

myself repeatedly being thrown away exclusively based on the fact I wasn't eager enough (or should we perhaps say *desperate enough*?), to answer *every* question and fulfil *every* request I was asked to. I went as far as being unmatched solely because, when asked about my college major, instead of instantly answering the question (I have three majors, and that's a complicated pathway to go down on a first interaction), I chose to say "That's a bit difficult to explain right now, can we talk about it later?" And, simply put, this is completely absurd, that an entire human being is discarded away for nothing else than tacitly refusing to answer one single question when prompted to.

At the same time, for women, usually seen as the main commodity of online media, anything goes. In fact, an additional experiment me and Helena once did, the one of creating a *female* profile on an online dating website, basically led us to a status similar to that of an untouchable virtual goddess – we hadn't even finished filling up the profile and we were already receiving multiple messages. Despite the fact the

---

potentially get one unresponsive match every month.

profile literally read "THIS PROFILE IS FAKE" (all in caps!), nobody would read it, and people would talk to us just as if that warning wasn't even there at all. Following that, we literally tried to violate all of the website's rules and terms of use, and we were only penalized *once*, *with a three-day ban and a request to stop doing it*, when we repeatedly told (male) users that we were minors, i.e. actually 17 instead of 18 years old.

This difference of treatments makes it very difficult for any real relationship to flourish, even more if we take into account how increasingly difficult it is becoming to connect to *one* person, to establish an effective and long dialogue with them. First, you need to be seen as super attractive; second, you need to sheepishly accept everything you're requested to do; third, you... well, that already goes beyond the scope of this book, but the essential part is that if you cannot seem attractive enough, the whole process quickly falls through and you won't even be able to establish a dialogue with anyone at all.

Realistically, the current environment of online

dating and relationships focuses on photos alone. You may be the most amazing man who has ever lived, you may even have an impeccably well written profile, but nobody seems to care about any of that these days. Instead, unless your photos are appetizing enough and you make yourself seem *very* attractive, there's absolutely no real chance for you to meet another human being. Unless you abide by those rules, you won't stand a single chance. You don't have to be specially ugly, you just have to be *anything* below an impossible greek god and you will barely stand a chance. And this, predictably, generates a lot of problems.

If you truly are a greek god, with the actual looks of a whole new Apollo, people will never believe you are yourself. Time and again, they will ask you for your social media, and either you have multiple profiles in almost every social network known to mankind, or you'll repeatedly be called a liar. I myself, at one point, had to digitally manipulate photos to "get verified" as a real person, and I had to create a fake *Instagram* account to present it as my own to those who requested it – doing all this is a complete waste of time, of course, but it only shows that if someone wants to present you with photos that are not his own, they can always find some way to do so and trick you.

If you are an average man, like I usually am, you will be constantly facing an unfair competition. It's like taking a pair of rollerblades to a Formula 1 competition – you may be able to win a race here and there, of course, but only if something truly unusual happens and all the best cars break down. So, why not even up the odds with the few tools you currently have available to you?

If you are a woman, you may be skipping perfectly amazing men just because you are, right now, constantly being fed the illusion there's something better, *way better*, out there. Instead, you could be meeting someone who isn't all that attractive, but who will actually be a great match for yourself, and who will truly give you all those things you feel are currently missing from your life. But you could also, of course, end up with a complete jerk – those exist, but the way they look does not hint at who they are, as the famous case of Ted Bundy easily proves.

So, simply put, why is it that creating a profile with fake photos ends up being a positive thing nowadays? Most of all, because not doing so will put you at an enormous disadvantage, and essentially make it impossible for you to talk to other people. Of course that, sooner or later, you'll have to reveal people the truth, and that's hard to do, but... do notice that unless you had lied in your photos in first place, you wouldn't even have gotten so far. It takes us all back to the original "Turtle" and "Hare" experiment, where you'll be stuck with the status of the former, and people will make the bare minimum effort in talking to you – that is, if they even do so. And this whole problem, although sad and disappointing, says a lot about today's world...

48

7- Final thoughts

Yes, if you were to see me in some online app or website, you'd quickly be facing "fake" photos, in the sense I'm not the person shown in any of them. And yet, I'm still a human being, I have feelings, and the option I have to take comes exclusively from the fact that we, nowadays, live in a society which increasingly, and most absurdly, cares more about static images and pure fantasies than it does about people's own personal achievements. Out of two people, one with a beautiful photo taken on a beach, and a second one who has earned multiple research awards and scholarships, people now care too much about the first and don't even pay a second look to the second.

It is crucially important to invert the pathway that today's society is taking. One's value should neither be seen by beautiful photos, nor by number of *likes* and *followers* they gather. One Kim Kardashian should not be seen as more desirable in our culture than the likes of Plato, Albert Einstein or Stephen Hawking. *Catfishing*, if we want to define as such the practise of presenting other people's photos online as if they were our own, is – in my personal opinion – not as much about hiding one's true identity, as it is about fulfilling a new cultural rule that requires people to adhere to completely impossible standards, and which decides to discard away, as mere trash (and often, barely human), those who fail to achieve that unbelievable standard.

Despite regretting what happened with Tatiana, since it is terrible to go out with a person who is expecting a "Hare" and gets a "Turtle", without being allowed to make such a choice based on truthful facts, I do not regret what I'll have to continue doing; instead, I find it profoundly disappointing that one currently has to live in a society such as the one described in here, in which people do generally enjoy talking to me, but would – apparently – never give me such a chance unless I had told them a single lie, a lie that I can't regret because, at the end of each day, it is a lie that is now required to succeed in establishing online relationships of any kind.

www.ingramcontent.com/pod-product-compliance
Lightning Source LLC
LaVergne TN
LVHW051618050326
832903LV00033B/4562